Gallery Books
Editor Peter Fallon

STATES

Ciaran Berry

STATES

Gallery Books

States
is first published
simultaneously in paperback
and in a clothbound edition
on 22 May 2025.

The Gallery Press
Loughcrew
Oldcastle
County Meath
Ireland

www.gallerypress.com

ISBN 978 1 91133 896 3 *paperback*
978 1 91133 897 0 *clothbound*

A CIP catalogue record for this book
is available from the British Library.

States receives financial assistance
from the Arts Council of Ireland.

the arts council an chomhairle ealaíon funding literature

Contents

States *page* 11
Dinoflagellates 14
The Castro Theatre 16
The Lavender Lighter 19
Poison Ivy 24
Astoria 27
The Harlem Tiger 30
The N for Never 33
The Last Days of the Amato Opera 36
La Cité des Enfants Perdus 39
Riverdale 43
I Am Legend 45
Photographs from the Exclusion Zone 48
Water Bear 50
Night of the Living Dead 53
Call Me, Ishmael 56
Shopping on eBay for Laika Memorabilia 59
Doctor Atomic 61
You & Me: The B-Movie 64
The Man Who Fell to Earth 68
Close Encounters 71
Roach 73
The Making of Jaws 75
Circus, Fire 78
Fresh Air 81
The Vegas Nerve 84
Guess Who's Coming to Dinner 87
Evel Knievel 90
The Comb Over 91
Eat the Peach 93

Acknowledgements and Notes 98

Interviewer: Tell me, how did you find America?
John Lennon: Turned left at Greenland.
— A Hard Day's Night

Bunny Kelly: Ah, States is brilliant!
Git Hynes: You been there?
Bunny Kelly: Yeah. Eh, no. Well, just on the telly, you know?
— I Went Down

States

Having turned left at Greenland
I end up here, just off the on-ramp
to I-84, in this, my this one-time-
at-band-camp sort of life, once
more moving around the furniture,
always in two minds, neither
of them my own, caught between places,
like the Colossus of Rhodes,
or Elvis, near the climax to 'Polk
Salad Annie', splitting his pants
as he drops into a karate stance.
I'll have what he's having — peanut
butter and grape jelly, banana
and bacon between two slices
of Texas toast, or what the hero
orders having entered an empty
diner in *The Twilight Zone* — eggs
over easy, coffee, hash browns,
and how he confides to the silence:
'See, there's some question about
my identity. Let me put it to you
this way, I'm not sure who I am.'

Snow banks on the East River seems
apt, amnesia and ping-pong,
and Allen Ginsberg waking up alone
on Market Street, not sure how
he got there with a military haircut
and a suitcase full of poems, or
how, on the answering machine
to the Irish Consulate, I hit playback
and hear a voice not quite my own
give my name and address, so that
I press erase and record again.

As in the ending to a child's story,
then I woke up and it was all
a dream — the hubbub and chutzpah
of this Connecticut suburb, these
lovely humans who call themselves
my wife and sons. If I click three
times these blue suede shoes. If,
under my breath, I whisper 'there's
no place like home', it's a country
& western hit I come upon,
all heartache and rhinestone.

It shifts from its slot in the jukebox;
across its worn down grooves
the needle skips as I step, once more,
into the falling snow of whatever
comes before the yellow alarm clock,
the fog-bound plane that, a day late,
tilts over forty shades of green,
bearing me towards the blue-gloved
border officer who almost breaks
my fingers as she inks me for a set
of prints, demanding irked that I
relax my hand. 'States is brilliant,'
as one ex-con on the run remarks
to his partner in *I Went Down*.
'One of us . . . One of us,' as, in *Freaks*,
the armless girl and bearded lady sing.
'Are you Irish at all?' as Davin puts it
to Stephen, 'what with your name
and your ideas?' What with Jacob
Steendam declaring, 'Oh, this is Eden,'
as his ship enters the Hudson, before
he steps aboard a downtown N?

Neither born here, nor of parents
born here, I stand clear of the closing
doors and try not to manspread
or mansplain about how, half-cut,
I stood on the wrong platform
and ended up in Queens, about how,
half the time at least, it feels as if
I'm the one called in to play the cello
in this marching band, having
turned left at Greenland, having,
with nothing to declare, passed through
Customs, and once more checking
the feng shui of the room, hearing
the tap, tap, tap and how d'you like that?
of our off, off-Broadway neighbour
in his studio apartment on the fifth floor
or, outside the Night Café,
those merry men of Gotham spinning a yarn
about some Johnny-come-lately
come to town, bearing on his shoulders,
to save his mount, a bushel
of wheat, or a basket of wampum.

Dinoflagellates

The synodic month is in its last quarter. In a moment,
    for the first time, we will kiss where the Pacific breaks
against the rocks of the Franciscan Complex, and
    the dinoflagellates protest the brush of wave and fish.

The water glows with them as in some B-movie
    in which the doors have opened on the just landed
ship, and we await our first glimpse of the alien.
    They self-expose like a man with nothing on

under his coat as, years before, you step aboard
    an uptown number 4, bound for Bedford Park
and Bronx Science. Or like that giant mirrorball
    of glass and steel from which *The Man from Planet X*

will soon reveal his *papier-mâché* head under
    its goldfish bowl helmet as he steps down
onto that fogbound Scottish island, where the locals
    speak in an accent that's pure Darby O'Gill.

The lights flick on and off as your train rattles
    up Lex and two boys set up shop to dance hip hop,
who, for all the world, could be those kids
    from *Fame* — Shaun Earl and Gene Anthony Ray

turning cartwheels through the cathode rays
    of my first black & white on a Tuesday night
just this side of The Angelus. As if spot- or
    strobe-lit, they break and pop, they pose and pirouette,

like these dinoflagellates waving their glow sticks
    as if they're dancers at an ocean rave, or the marshaller
whose signals will guide my plane to the right gate
    the morning I touch down at JFK to meet you,

once more, at the baggage claim, in my right hand
        a note in comic sans that insists you take me to your leader,
or at least the Family Fun Center, where I'll challenge
        that famous chicken to a game of tic-tac-toe.

Why don't you be X and I'll be O, as, later, you'll be X
        to the Y chromosome that will settle the sex of our two
space cadets, already suiting up to board their ship
        to where we are? I'm the cross-border representative

on one of those 'take them out of the Troubles' trips,
        and you're the goat girl for whom my heart is doing
backflips, like those boys working in perfect stereo
        in their Adidas high tops as, in spite of all those

poles and passengers, they move, seamlessly,
        from the windmill to the cricket and the armchair
to the flare, to the ever more intricate scratch
        and mix of Jam Master Jay, is it? or Grandmaster Flash.

The Castro Theatre

The show wasn't over until the Wurlitzer rose up out of
  the floor,
    nor without that organ could the show begin.
      Check out
the leatherette ceiling, the art-deco chandelier in this, my
  bluffer's guide

    to the interior. Thank you, Wikipedia, now if you
      could just help me
remember what we were there for? A rerun of *Across the
  Continent*?
    A *Rocky Horror* singalong? Once more I play charades
      with Mnemosyne.

She holds one finger up, then taps it with two others off
  her arm.
    Of course! It was Emir Kusturica's *Underground*,
      Yugoslavia coming
undone right in front of the lens in what Slavoj Žižek
  dismisses

    as a horrible film. It was mid-March of 1998, the
      early days
of my Johnny-just-off-the-boat, Johnny-come-lately phase,
  though
    really I was Johnny just off the plane. BA flight 2870,
      to be precise.

In our basement sublet, headlights turned one wall to a
  blank screen
    onto which I now project that fleet of Messerschmidts
      about to drop
their payload on the Belgrade Zoo. It's early April 1941,
  month

of my mother's birth, the Belfast Blitz. A goose
pecks at a tiger.
Silly goose! The tiger bites. From a window ledge, an
escaped
elephant pilfers a pair of patent leather shoes. You're
talking

in your sleep again, ringing someone up at Green Apple,
where
once you rang up Robin Williams (Nanu! Nanu!), or
discussing
the fog on a crosstown bus. The doors hiss and we step
aboard

the 38 Geary or the 24 Divisadero. The bellows of the
accordion
open and close, and I slip through a loose-latched Hopper
window.
Raccoon-masked, I root back through our things.
Clothes hung to dry

over an upturned bicycle. A borrowed copy of Ted
Hughes's *Wodwo*:
'What am I? Nosing here.' Our year of living under-
ground no more
than a Muni pass, a pack of Marlboro. Check out my
corduroys,

this chevron-patterned shirt — exactly the sort of
thing Marko
and Blacky wouldn't cut up for curtains as they rollick
and romp
through *Once Upon a Time There Was a Country*, as
the film, once,

was known. There's feasting. There's dancing. There's a pool cue
twisted round a necktie and turned into a weapon. But, after a while,
the subtitles are insufficient, the cast divides as if by binary fission.

I get lost in the spectacle and miss the allegory. Once upon a time
there was a country in which you and I . . . You know the rest, my love.
My ill-fitting thrift-store suit. Your drop-waist dress. Our stammered

vows on a windswept beach in February. And back in the movie
palace of it now, the carpet still sticky beneath our feet. Our mouths
all grease and husk from the popcorn that runs out somewhere

around a wedding scene as unlikely as ours — the bride wheeled
in on a metal contraption that makes it look, but not really, as if
she's flying. The groom giddy with what he hopes will happen soon.

The Lavender Lighter

Who knew that, in order to better hold a tune,
Ol' Blue Eyes would swim laps under water
in a piano-shaped pool? Or that Charles Spencer
Chaplin, as his mother might, irate, have
called him from time to time, first appeared
on stage as one of eight clog-dancing lads
from Lancashire? Who knew that you
and I would still be here twenty years
after we left the party and never came back
with the beer? Who knows if it was Sierra
Nevada or Anchor Steam we'd been sent out for
that year before the first of many years
in which we lived, like Captain Beefheart
and his Magic Band, off soybeans, government
surplus cheese, you stacking shelves
in Green Apple, while I sifted the clutter
down the back of Harringtons — a single
wooden crutch, a box of scratched LPs,

a concrete Buddha whose laughter seemed
to set in motion his belly's many rings,
and who seemed to be laughing at you
and me. Was it Heineken perhaps, or
'fuck that shit, Pabst Blue Ribbon' as Frank
Booth puts it in *Blue Velvet* before ducking
behind his mask for another draw of helium?
I keep going back to the scene where
Jeffrey Beaumont comes across a human ear.
I keep going back to the scene where
Dorothy Vallens appears naked at his door,
desperate to be taken in, as with those
huddled masses of Emma Lazarus, of whom
I was and wasn't one, looking down
on cloud shapes straight out of *The Simpsons*
on my way to SFO, where the carousel

        spits out my father's canvas Karrimor.
    With it on his back, he climbed Pen

y Fan and Glyder Fach. With it on his back,
    he climbed Scafell Pike and Skiddaw.
    Now I take it up and walk with you,
once more, to our first of four sublets
at a Potrero Hill commune. We lie together
    where, for background noise, it's Cowboy
Junkies or Psychic TV. We lie together
        where, for background noise, a boy spins
    doughnuts in a souped-up coupé. Sometimes
the cops seal off the projects behind us.
    Sometimes I'm the last white face on the bus.
    And though something here seems to suggest
this ode's an elegy it's not as I hit fast forward
or rewind on a mix you made me once of Luscious
    Jackson, Digable Planets and Fishbone.
As I dial all of our old numbers to see if
        we're at home at 25th between Wisconsin
    and Connecticut, or 14th between Valencia

and Guerrero, or whatever the address
    at which we did our best to live up to
    the contents of our letters, our end of century
epistolary romance, all the dollars you
spent on airmail stamps of aviation pioneers —
    Jacqueline Cochran with her 'Wings for Britain',
Eddie Rickenbacker with his Croix de Guerre.
        I didn't know then that a set of forceps,
    poorly wielded by the OBGYN, would leave
the newborn Francis Albert Sinatra with
    a scar on his left cheek, a burst eardrum,
    or that his father fought in the bantamweight
division under the pseudonym Marty O'Brien,

Italians not yet being welcome in the world
of boxing. Nor did I know that Chaplin's mother,
Hannah, would meet her future husband
(also Charles) during rehearsals for
a production of *Shamus O'Brien* (no relation).

I didn't know the N Judah from the 2 Clement,
or the Elixir from The Bitter End, as I pulled the cord
on the accordion bus and, in my London
Fog coat, stepped down into the fog that would
soon burn off to reveal the sky's electric blue;
as I pulled the cord on the accordion bus
and stepped off under a sky the colour of bruised
flesh or bruised fruit in an El Niño year.
In the Western Union the cashier holds my cheque
up to the light to read the watermark and we
do our best to keep our heads above water.
Nothing in the fridge but brewer's yeast
and tahini. Nothing in the fridge but kimchi
and bok choy. In Pacifica houses slip into
the Pacific and you bring me pirozhki
from the Russian bakery on Geary, as I bring you
flowers from behind the funeral home.
An earthquake shakes the windows

of Crossroads Trading, and I don't know
whether to stay put or run, just as I didn't know
that Charles Junior once played the part
of Billy the pageboy in *Sherlock Holmes*.
And who knew that Irwin Allen Ginsberg —
pulling on a deerstalker perhaps, drawing
on a calabash — would mimic Chaplin's walk
as he felt for the feet of his long line? I may
have made this up, I may have got it wrong
from your copy of the Miles biography,

which I read at my desk without a drawer,
a short ride crosstown on the 22 Fillmore
from where, at the Six Gallery, Ginsberg
read 'Howl' out loud before a crowd
for the first time. And didn't we, too, see the best
mimes of our generation feeling
for a pane of glass that wasn't there,
that year you taught me the Yiddish

for go peddle your fish elsewhere, which
seems apt given my cod and my kipper,
my flounder and stingray forever
stinking up the place? Among our roommates,
a runaway Mormon wife who looked you
too long in the eye, a supply teacher
who liked to jump freight trains. And on the way
to school, from that Hoboken tenement,
the other kids yelling 'Dago' at Sinatra
and throwing stones. And Chaplin, on his last day
in the country, making devil horns before
the lens of Richard Avedon. '*Amach an doras*,'
as my old boss used to say, his second
favourite phrase after 'Talk is cheap but
it takes money to buy whiskey,' something
we knew well that year of Salvation Army
sheets and mismatched cutlery, of stained
mattresses and half-burned-out TVs,

as, like a couple of extras, a couple of
hangers on, from *The Tramp* perhaps,
or *The Vagabond*, we trudged towards this
uncertain future presided over by a character
straight out of *The Great Dictator*, who might
yet show every one of us the door. Who knew
it would come to this? I didn't know, although

I like to think Frédéric Auguste's sculpture,
on which are etched the words of that daughter
of Moses and Esther — whose name suggests
we might yet rise from the dead unscathed,
if not unscarred — holds in her right hand
not the tiki torch that, of late, has burned
through every truth we held to be self-evident,
and therefore dear, but instead the lavender
lighter you or I swiped by accident, one
night, from The Pig and Whistle, was it?
No, it was The Plough and the Stars.

Poison Ivy

Those four part harmonies, the riff's rinse and repeat
and, suddenly,
a Sunday at Muir Beach where I'm dragging tree
stumps to the teeth
of the splitter. Eucalyptus or Locust, maybe Douglas Fir.
And I'm back

here for the wit of your letters and this 1959 hit
from The Coasters,
which, according to the lyricist, might be a metaphor for
an STD.
You ask me if I've ever heard of Iowa, if, when it
comes to sea glass,

I prefer blue or green. You quote Jean Toomer from 'the
best book
ever', something about the heart and the full moon. I
take the 130
from Mission & 5th again, then I extend my thumb on
Highway 1.

I make small talk in the cab of a Ford Bronco. The
driver's people
were from Cahirsiveen. And it's not figurative, but literal
what
I'll carry home with me, like aniseed in a story my
grandfather

told me about a thief trying to lure away a dog of pedigree.
'Poison
Ivy, Poison Ivy,' those four singers intone, live from
the Horseshoe
or the Apollo, all synchronized handclaps and finger clicks
as I drag

these lopped limbs from the undergrowth. Bay
Laurel, I'm thinking,
or maybe Coast Live Oak. In their flamingo suits they
step back
from the microphones, twirl once between the chorus
and middle-

eight. Later, one of them will be shot through the wind-
shield of his
Buick before a comeback at the Lady Luck. Later, one
of them will
barely avoid a pauper's grave. I'm all tangled up in the
weeds of it

again, scent of sage brush and, no, it can't be mesquite,
and the guy
I'm working beside telling me about a wedding where he
passed
a joint to Yasmine Bleeth, and how last week he got into
a fist fight

over a parking space on Clement between 7th & 8th. The
screech
of the machine reminds me of Robert Frost, just as
California used
to conjure The Beach Boys and Baywatch, Mitch Buchannon
with

his torpedo buoy and tan from a can. I'm working my
way back
to the gist of it again, what we'll pass between us later, limb
to limb,
my skin unblemished though yours will rash and burn,
your letters

so much more eloquent than mine, asking if I see in the moon a rabbit
or a human face, or if I know the difference between a sweet potato
and a yam. 'Poison Ivy, Poison Ivy,' those Coasters sing again before

they're ripped off by The Beatles and The Stones. And, like I said,
it's not a metaphor here, or at least it isn't yet. I reek of stale sweat
and other people's cigarettes. I'm on the bus back to our second

sublet. My head hitting the glass as I dose off. The diesel engine's heave
and susurrus. And so much that's new to me, such as this plant, three
leaflets to a leaf I carry back to you on the cuffs of my ill-fitting jeans.

Astoria

It's the realtor with the walleye I picture, the backseat of
his Buick,
a royal pine Little Tree above the dash. Then it's our
super — a Bosnian
refugee with a beanie hat and a luxurious moustache —
as he sorts
the recycling from the trash. It's our landlord's
insomniac son I see,

recently divorced, and treading the boards of his floor
and our ceiling
at 4 a.m. It's Saturday morning, then it's Sunday
afternoon, coffee
and oranges, and the couple next door at it again: 'You
stabbed me
with a knife! Look at my fucking hand!' And a
neighbour answers

'I'm calling the police.' There's a leak above us, so
the bathroom
light fixture fills with water like a goldfish bowl. I hit
the switch
before I notice; the bulb explodes. There's nothing
on at the Sixplex,
so we sit through *Deuce Bigalow* in which Amy
Poehler's character,

Ruth, has Tourette's: 'Ball sweat! Anus! Scrotum! Shove
it up your ass!'
I'm walking backwards like a sideshow geek, if not
biting the head
off the chicken, then at least ordering, by accident, the
chicken's feet.
The menu's in Spanish, and I don't speak even a
poquito. Ask me,

instead, about how I lugged home, through snow, a refurbished TV/
VCR combo in the heyday of Blockbuster Video, twenty copies
of *The Matrix* and every one already out on loan. Ask me instead
about the ageing *theíos* in nothing but a Speedo, climbing from his Volvo

to waddle towards the deep end of Astoria Park Pool. Did you know
that this part of the borough was known as Hallett's Cove until John
Jacob Astor made a shitload off beaver fur and selling opium to
the Chinese? That Astoria is the name of a Tony Bennett album

and Waldorf's wife in *The Muppet Show*, the one we never see?
I left my heart in San Francisco, then I followed it here to fall asleep,
on your birthday in the cheap seats at *Kiss Me, Kate* or *Annie, Get*
Your Gun, to take my shoes off on the landing the day we moved

in above Mr and Mrs Kim. Here she is, bringing to our door six
un-shucked ears of corn, and when she says 'You cook' you're not
sure if it's a question or an instruction. Here she is off to the First
Korean Church in a transit van covered in Hangul script. Here's that

lost tourist, a pack of Marlboro tucked into the sleeve of his white Tee,
as he tells me I speak English 'real well', before asking which platform
he should stand on to get the hell out of Queens. 'Love It Or Leave It',
a sign threatens in the window of the blinds store, setting up your joke

about the blind leading the blind, and the same advice we would find
later on a piece of sheet music written by Joseph F Weber of Scranton,
PA, who wants me to go back where I belong. I like to picture him with
John Rocker on the 7 out to Shea, where it's game five of the 'degenerates'

against the Braves. I like to picture him as a Guardian Angel stepping
from car to car in a red bomber jacket and a red beret, the rough hand
that shakes me awake in my tartan party pants, among the lost, busy
sleeping one off, far from you my love, and a long way past my stop.

The Harlem Tiger

To see it for the first time through a hole drilled in the door, or in the crosshairs
of the sharpshooter — this creature named for the second Han emperor, or Flash
Gordon's merciless nemesis, who once again poses a threat to Planet Earth.

It's 1980 and Prince Vultan leads his hawk men towards the Imperial Palace
while Flash rides beside him on an airborne jet ski. Or it's 2003 and you work
the treadle of the sewing machine, making the costume you'll wear on Halloween.

'Seatbelts, please,' they ham it up on the front page of the *Times* as news
breaks of Antoine Yates and his roommate with a taste for chicken thighs,
though this part-time cab driver will later confide that bringing up a tiger

'wasn't no different than raising a monkey or a snake'. Let's say he walks it
in the park at night and that, once, on the feast of Saint Francis he takes it
to the Cathedral of Saint John the Divine, this pussy cat straight out of Blake

that, in the *Songs of Experience*, puts a shape on the sublime. How bright
it burns in the eyes of the marksman, who rappels from the seventh floor
for a sightline. How bright in our cramped one bedroom apartment as you

guide the black and amber of the fur fabric towards
the needle's rapid fire,
shaping this simulacrum you'll wander in from bar to
bar. Pins cushioned
between your lips, I wonder if you're not the spit of
your maternal grandfather

come from Hungary to his tailor's window on the Upper
East Side, where
he too guides the seam into the machine, as if feeding
a beast with teeth
the size of thumbs and a tongue so rough it can scrape the
meat off its prey.

In the Royal Cinema in Limerick, or the Carlton
maybe, Freddie Mercury
hits the high notes in the theme tune, and my cousin and I
boo the villain
with the Fu Manchu moustache. We await the climax
where, impaled

on his own rocket, Ming's blood runs green, while up on
the fifth floor
of the Drew Hamilton Houses, that apex predator
paces the sitting room,
so seemingly at home it's as if it's looking for the crossword
or the remote.

The dart settles in its rump, the tiger snarls and turns,
and the shooter
lingers at the end of his rope. Whatever 'operates in a
manner analogous
to terror' is just one way Edmund Burke names the
sublime. And Blake

tapping trochees on the tabletop, trying to settle all that
muscle into lines.
And you and I riding the 1 downtown with Richard
Simmons and Olivia
Newton-John, our carriage so kitsch and ridiculous it's
as if we're in that

scene from the film where, with just seconds left to
save this obscure body
in the S K System, Ming makes to marry an earthling,
taking Dale to be his
empress of the hour. Like you, she's a New York girl
as out of place on Planet

Mongo as that dolphin that shows up in the Gowanus
Canal, or the tiger that,
by now, they've laid out on a stretcher and borne, in
silence, towards the elevator,
and tucked into the bed of the box truck they'll use to
ship it off to Noah's Ark.

The N for Never

You step over a Jackson Pollock of pigeon
shit towards where, by the raised platform,
the line goes *snap*. Like Walter Benjamin's
angel of history, you face backwards into
a future you arrive at stop by stop.
You're wearing khakis long after Labor Day
and these wide-collared shirts that say
'ready to party'. You bought them at the
Salvation Army on Steinway, where a rat
dragged its sorry ass between the racks
of everything long fallen out of fashion,
of everything mismatched and a magnet
for hair from the pair of cats you
and your wife have taken in — refugees from
a friend's apartment fire, one named
the Russian for little bear, the other after
a New York Liberty basketball player.
You're new to this place by the water
bought and sold for a handful of kettles,
axes, awls, a jaw harp, a bolt of cloth.
New and nowhere near cool enough
for the hipsters in their winklepicker shoes
as you sink under the foam of your headphones
and then under the foam of the East River,
where it's Gene Autry, then The Pogues,
Luke Kelly and Nina Simone. You think
of Marilyn Monroe's white dress rising
in the rush of air rising towards Lex
as she and Tom Ewell exit *Creature*
from the Black Lagoon, and of a sandhog
stepping from a man lock, as if stepping
out of a submarine — one of Emerson's
immigrant millions with too much guano
in his destiny. What would he make
of you in your orange seat, praised by

the American Posture League for how
it fits the contours of the human form,
as, heart hepped up on too much caffeine,
you make your way to Credit Suisse
First Boston, where they pay you to answer
a phone that never rings while the actress
in the next cubicle tries out lines
from *A Streetcar Named Desire*? She wants
the part of Blanche, but who doesn't?
You're late again — the N for never lives
up to its name. It comes and goes
like those mole people rumoured hereabouts
to poke their heads up out of holes,
or those old selves of ours that settle
in the second person, only to surface later
as in a game of Whac-a-Mole. Down
at Federal Plaza they've lost your papers
and so you'll take a ticket and stand in line
as if waiting for a quarter of Bologna
or Serrano ham. Your wife will call in a favour
from an old friend who'll call in one
from a congressman the future
will remember for the photographs he sends
to a porn star and a blackjack dealer
of his 'man-bulge in boxer briefs', and
all this flux will start to feel like home.
Doctor Zizmor has a cure for your acne
that comes ten years too late, ten years
before he retires to study the Talmud,
and there's a 1-800 number for a lawyer
who'll chase your ambulance
at a reasonable rate. That's your reflection
in the glass, or someone else's going
the other way. Go on, give us a wave,
as cradle-rocked or all shook up

like the gin in a gimlet, you get lost again
between Ditmas and Mermaid.

The Last Days of the Amato Opera

No matter where we lived those years there was always
  an opera singer
    a few blocks over practising her scales, working her
      way, let's say, towards
an aria from Da Ponte's troubled take on a troubled tale.
  Somewhere,

    somebody hits a high note on the keyboard, or the
      needle skips towards
the overture and I'm back in my seat on the Bowery for
  the Sunday matinee.
    Your childhood best friend's roommate is playing
      one of the Donnas, though

I can't remember which, just as I can't find a record of
  this performance,
    part of a run that lasted just one weekend. When I
      go back to it, it's as if
I'm looking out the window of a train at a wrecking-
  balled building,

    the floral wallpaper on the last wall standing of a
      room on the third
floor, a door that opens into nothing and nowhere. When
  I go back to it
    it's Bernard Malamud writing 'In New York who
      needs an atom bomb?

If you walked away from a place they tore it down.' The
  scene's like
    any of our short lease apartments, meaning the
      orchestra has room
for the piano and the pianist, but never both at the same
  time, meaning

what was once rent controlled will soon be gutted
for condos —
exposed brick and stainless steel appliances, a chef's
station, a Miele
espresso machine. For now, though, I'm high again
on the paint fumes

from those backdrops that would spirit us to Spain and
the last days
of the Hapsburg reign which, in spite of warfare,
famine and plague,
is the perfect playground for the libertine. Of his
conquests of city girl

and country girl, he sings. Of his conquests of
countess and baroness.
There's his little black book (his libretto!) tied up with a
string bow.
There's a wing of pheasant, a glass of Marzemino.
There's you and me

in the fifth row the year after we elope, called in once
more to add
to the applause and bring the flowers (half a dozen
orange bodega
roses wrapped in cellophane) and still we've no idea what's
going on.

So much of it gets lost in translation, so much of it
happens backstage
or between scenes, like this one in which Leporello and
Don Giovanni
exchange clothes outside Donna Elvira's window, or
this one, where

the cast and crew smoke Lucky Strikes or Newports by the concourse
of the gas station next door. Like that blue rinse old dear who, in search
of a restroom, wanders in bewildered from the wings, I turn up my collar

and step again through the oatmeal confetti that falls, like unexpected snow,
at the wedding of Zerlina and Masetto, what I at best half-remember held
together with Scotch tape and Velcro, with safety pins and string, like

this ramshackle show from the last days of the Amato, in which Antonio
himself plays the Commendatore, come back out of the grave to drag
the villain through a trapdoor in the stage floor and down into the flames.

La Cité des Enfants Perdus

Marc Caro and Jean-Pierre Jeunet, 1995

It sounds better in French — a language you don't speak and one
I barely understand, squinting to keep track of the subtitles in
our fifth floor walk-up on Amsterdam and 106th, where, as the tape
shifts from supply to take up reel, you predict one day you'll give birth

to a son the spit of the strongman's little brother cum-sidekick,
around whom so much of this story spins. A city of lost children.
A scientist who means to make off with their dreams. A carnival
where the crusher of bones will try, once more, to shatter steel.

It's the scene where a giant flea lowers its hi-vis proboscis
into the scalp of a conjoined twin, or the scene where the frogman,
in his brass and copper finery, wanders forlorn on the bottom
of a green sea — two moments I carry with me as I wax the legs

of our bed with Vaseline to keep at bay the *Cimex lectularius*
(it sounds better in Latin). They congregate in the cracks where

the floorboards are coming up like track in this railroad
we rent
for a pittance. Once more we try to sleep, perchance
to dream,

but it's impossible, as it is for that quack who straps the
snatched boy
into the sarcophagus and makes to wander through
his subconscious.
The snow falls on the snowman. The toy soldier crashes
his cymbals,
and suddenly the room is full of Santa Clauses.
'Alleluia, Alleluia'

the man who waves his bible up and down the avenue all
hours
begins to sing. 'Jesus, he lives,' and we wake to a
fresh set of welts
where the bedbugs have whispered their *Je t'aime*. It's
February.
We drag our books in refuse sacks up to the tar
beach roof to freeze,

and when we leave we jettison our furniture, but your
prophesy
I carry with me until the night years later when I
bring round
the car, one thing having led to another, as in that sequence
that
begins with a shed tear and ends with a cargo ship
splitting the pier.

In between, a gull shits on the windshield of a Model-T
that upends

the fire hydrant that gives rise to the flood on which
three rats,
on a tea tray, careen downstream. Cause and effect
beginning
with the infinitesimal, if in Beijing a monarch flaps
its wings

is not what I'm thinking, because I'm not thinking as
I forget
the lights and you ride shotgun, swearing this isn't it,
as if
our little cosmonaut were not strapped into his ship and
soon
to join us in our '93 Camry. It's Easter Sunday. 'Jesus,
he lives,'

our old neighbour sings in his ecstasy, swinging his
leather-bound.
At Saint Luke's you waddle weighed down towards
the maternity wing,
where round noon our Yuri Gagarin will enter this atmo-
sphere,
gasping for oxygen. I'll love the way he mixes up his
Ps and Ks,

how he yells 'ball,' pointing at a full moon. I'll love him
in our new
sitting room, dancing loose-limbed to The Strokes. As
the song goes
it's hard to explain. A boy burps into the camera and,
seven years
before he's born, you see our son. Krank's laboratory
is blown sky-

high in an explosion of conical flasks and gas syringes
from which
Miette and One get the kids out just in time. In a car
so old it's become
a joke in *The Onion* we take him home, this boy we'll
raise to go
in fear of the Cyclops and the Octopus with its
manifold arms.

Riverdale

I'm sitting across from you in the Broadway Diner,
where the agèd regulars remind me of rowers,
raising their spoons, as if they weighed
the same as oars, from bowls
of matzo ball and minestrone. I'm sitting across
from you in the Broadway Diner, where it's eggs
over easy with a side of rye. We are ten years
into this choose your own adventure,
which is neither *The Lost Jewels of Nabooti* nor
The Cave of Time. On our tabletop jukebox,
it's The Mamas & the Papas, then it's the Stray
Cats or Patsy Cline.

I've taken another inch off my IKEA desk so it'll fit
in the corner of a new room. I've filled out another
change of address form so Tom Ridge
will know exactly where I am — keeping
my voice low in *An Beal Bocht Cafe*
so as not to play a game of 'where you from?'
Watching the cricketers in the park, named
for George Clinton's lieutenant, crouch
at silly mid off or silly mid on. Forgive me a quip
about Parliament-Funkadelic. Forgive me a quip
about the mother ship. Our tête-à-tête, which
had fallen to silence,

like a phone going dead at one end of the line,
sputters to life as we barter baby names.
How about Moon Unit? How about
Spartacus? On the jukebox
it's Bill Haley & his Comets. On the jukebox
it's James Brown & the Famous Flames.
Later, I'll take three trains to Queens,
where I'm trying to teach *A Portrait of*

the Artist as a Young Man. I have read
little and understood less. Later, you'll tend to
high school kids at risk of the comma splice,
the split infinitive.

Then, on our 1-800-Mattress, we'll practise
some strange math. But now here comes
the waitress with her carafes. She tries
to point us towards the display case,
recommends the carrot cake, lemon meringue.
On the jukebox it's Gladys Knight &
the Pips. On the jukebox it's Diana Ross
& the Supremes. What about Elvis?
What about Dedalus? Or maybe Icarus?
Later, the oocyte and the blastocyst,
the plastic stick that gives rise to those two
pink lines. Later,

the transducer hovering over your midriff
like something out of *Space and Beyond*.
A child is a gift from God, our neighbour, John,
insists as beneath your winter coat
you start to show. A boy, the *abuelas*
in the elevator predict, based on the fact
that you're carrying low. And so we begin
our journey *By Balloon to the Sahara*. So we
fulfil the *Forecast from Stonehenge*. On
the jukebox it's Dick Dale & the Del Tones.
On the jukebox it's The Ink Spots
or The Four Tops.

I Am Legend

Francis Lawrence, 2007

What pretty pictures it makes, this nemesis that has us
soaping our hands
to dust. It's ink splotches various shades of blue, or
circles of clove rock
cut through like bone on butcher block. It's this spiked
rubber ball from
a paper bag of schlock one of our sons brings back
from a kid's party.

And I'm thinking now of the day we watched that troupe
of extras race
down 5th and through the arch from which George
Washington stares
out of the Tuckahoe marble. Tonight, watching the film
for the first time,
I have to wait until almost the last scene to find those
actors, transformed

by some cinematic sleight of hand to these grotesques, all
shaved heads
and translucent skin as they close in on that red-brick
brownstone,
where the Fresh Prince is a long way from Bel-Air. Of
course the plot
is terrible, but I get sidetracked by the spectacle of
New York like Pripyat

after the blast — all fallout and aftermath through which
Will Smith
joyrides across town in a Shelby Mustang, scattering
the starlings,

11th onto 57th, and 57th over to 6th? And so we're asked to believe
that this is how we'll fare when the weeds poke through the asphalt

of the fire lane and herds of deer wander about Times Square, when
our German Shepherds turn flesh eater in our arms and no one climbs
or descends the subway stairs. Take nine or ten, and the actors turn
and do it all again. The ping-pong balls on their speed skater suits

are markers by which the digital artist will track their movements
through space and time, as I join the dots here to retrace mine
to the car dealership where, this afternoon, as I waited for an oil
change, Doctor Phil, live from quarantine, consoled a pink-slipped

waitress somewhere in Queens. We blame the camel and the civet cat,
the horseshoe bat that no longer brings us any luck, and yet isn't this
what we really wanted all along, what with our weapons stockpiles
and our zombie flicks? We, who thought we were more than a blip

in the fourteen billion years of this universe? In one scene Smith

hits golf balls off a jet fighter aboard the USS *Intrepid*.
In another
he murmurs 'Please, say hello to me' into a mannequin's
cold ear.
And of course he gets to die like a hero, saving a
woman and child

from that horde of Darkseekers, who sit between gaping
mouth
vampires and Jar Jar Binks in *Complex* magazine's
countdown
of the least special effects in the history of film. Plane tree
leaves fall
into the dry fountain the city will spend millions to
move a few feet

east, and we choose to believe the production assistant
who insists
we must stay put and *shhhhh* until they've nailed the
shot, canned
the raw footage that will give rise to the final composite of
what attacks
the townhouse across the way, all steroidal vein and
apocalyptic rage.

Photographs from the Exclusion Zone

The prevailing scientific view of the exclusion zone has become that it is an unintentional wildlife sanctuary. This conclusion rests on the premise that radiation is less harmful to wildlife populations than we are.

— Mary Mycio, *Slate*

1

Here, in the long shadow of the sarcophagus,
we start to see what it would look like without us.
A Ferris wheel rusts in a stand of silver birch.
Through bumper cars weeds work their filigree.
The funfair is over; now it's the disaster movie.
The Assistant Director asks for quiet on the set
as the camera pans over the silenced reactor.
In the People's Park a statue of Vladimir Ilyich
reaches an arm towards nothing in particular.
Footprints of the roe deer score the latest snow.
The Przewalski's horse comes back, so too the boar
in spite of the numbers on the Geiger counter,
and the world gets back to what it was before.
It's like something straight out of a sci-fi script,
as if we're Laika, stepping aboard *Sputnik*,
leaving these grey tower blocks, all Brutalist.
In the abandoned ward so many empty cots.
In the shuttered theatre so many broken chairs.
What was it we thought we were doing here?
How did we ever come to think this place was ours?

2

How did we ever come to think this place was ours?
   What was it we thought we were doing here?
In the shuttered theatre so many broken chairs.
   In the abandoned ward so many empty cots.
Leaving these grey tower blocks, all Brutalist,
   as if we're Laika, stepping aboard *Sputnik*,
it's like something straight out of a sci-fi script.
   And the world gets back to what it was before.
In spite of the numbers on the Geiger counter,
   the Przewalski's horse comes back, so too the boar.
Footprints of the roe deer score the latest snow.
   Reaching an arm towards nothing in particular,
in the People's Park, a statue of Vladimir Ilyich.
   As the camera pans over the silenced reactor
the Assistant Director asks for quiet on the set.
   The funfair is over; now it's the disaster movie.
Through bumper cars weeds work their filigree.
   A Ferris wheel rusts in a stand of silver birch
and we start to see what it would look like without us,
   here, in the long shadow of the sarcophagus.

Water Bear

AKA moss piglet or tardigrade,
minute Christ with a blank face
and two black eyes. When the stone
rolls back from the sepulchre
you will survive even the meteor,
the gamma ray, rising into the not-
quite-afterlife like the lost wife
in *Revenge of the Zombies* whose
husband means to reanimate
the Reich, while we go the way
of the cave lion, the sloth lemur,
the great auk and the auroch,
the Atlas bear. Like a cannon
in khakis it says here, a sleeping
bag with legs, though what I see
is more pupa or chrysalis,
or even, yes, the foetus in utero
and up there on the screen
when the nurse sweeps
the transducer through goop
and grease and says, 'Look
away now if you don't wish
to learn the sex.' That plus
Robert Ettinger's Immortalists,
veins filled with antifreeze.
Our cryonics and the cold wish
they reveal — that we too might
survive the desert and the substrate
ooze, awakening from the deep
sleep of the deep freeze to a gin
resistant liver, the helicopter
as common as the family car.
Endurance artists
like the illusionist inside a block
of ice in Times Square, or a glass

coffin on the Upper West Side.
The headline: *Buried Alive*
On Riverside Drive, and there
he lies, like a saint with paper
skin in permanent repose.
The door to the crypt swings
open, the door to the crypt
swings closed. After the going
under we want to come back up,
like Dr von Altermann's
zombie assistant, whose name —
yes, you've guessed it — is Lazarus.
'Do you have a death wish?'
Oprah asks our illusionist.
'No, no, no, no,' he protests,
'the opposite!' On her show
he enters the Guinness Book
of World Records for holding,
under water, his breath, practising
something called static apnoea.
The pulse slows, the blood
abandons the extremities
to feed the heart and brain,
and, Christ, how it pains us
that we go the way of the root
vole, the golden mole, the red
gazelle, as far as ever from
Ettinger's golden age, in which,
whether frozen or thawed,
we come to see these fields,
woods, streams as *us*. Wee
tim'rous beastie, you are no more
than the mark a sharpened pencil
makes while we, it seems,
are the full stop at the end

of our sentence on this planet
where no spaceships come
to take us home. Broken down
to almost nothing but your DNA
under a rock in the Sinai, or falling
in a sudden shower of rain,
you're proof that, once set
in motion, life is hard to snuff,
although we do our best,
don't we, water bear? We try.

Night of the Living Dead

George A Romero, 1968

And so, once more, we end up here among the superstitious villagers,
something in the leaves astir, some heavy step that this way tends,
hoofed or steel-toed as the soundtrack skips from disco to dissonance,

and the moon kliegs a path through swamp or moor. Stiff of gait, this
grave creature, arisen straight-backed from the crypt of conjecture,
which in '68 brings us the flesh eater, arms out-stretched, tongue thick

with the grunt and murmur of what was once language as it draws
towards the TV's bluish flicker, or tries a brick against the window
of the car. As 'parable' is how the director describes horror, and so

I wonder what he'd make of this plague year, in which some of us
take to the root cellar while others continue to risk it up the stairs.
Aujourd'hui, maman est morte, someone suggests for an opening line

that captures the gist of the times, but my money's on this brother
and sister who've driven from Pittsburgh to tend their father's grave.

'You think I want to blow Sunday on a scene like this?' the son

exclaims, waving a gloved hand in the direction of the headstones
as YouTube counts down to an advert in 5, 4, 3, 2, 1. Later, he'll return
without his glasses on, one of the undead, who come club-footed

or bandy-legged across the lawn. In a black suit ripped at the arm
they come. In a bathrobe, a cocktail dress, a hospital gown, while,
like bog bodies, the culled mink of Jutland rise from their mass

grave and that ex-condo salesman, with the comb-over coiffure
and spray-on tan, pens his love letter to Hydroxychloroquine. We
read the newsfeed as if it were tealeaves, or the entrails the ghouls

will soon scarf down — liver and kidneys brought onto set for the extras
along with boxes of pizza, kegs of cheap beer. In gingham or denim
they appear. Buck naked, or in unbuttoned button downs, wanting

the heat of us, the sweet street meat of us spiked on its skewer
of bone, like this pathogen that turns the lungs to honey-comb, that

brings the night sweats and the cytokine storms. Our
food supplies

are low and, behind the mask, the mouth and nose become
obscene.
We stare into some *mise en scène* we have no context
for, slipping out
round dusk to the package store, waxing nostalgic for all
we did and

didn't do in the before. 'We urge you to stay tuned
and stay indoors,'
advises the newsman on the radio, while on the TV an
expert insists
the bereaved ought to forego 'the dubious comforts
of a funeral service'

to the accompaniment of another pop up window. On
Blairsville they
bear down, on Willard and Latrobe, as the algorithm
to my browsing
history tries to sell me Brooks running shoes, a Chevrolet,
VRBO.

Call Me, Ishmael

Turns out we loved our small lives after all — the banter
at the water cooler,
the cushion on the swivel chair, the office where,
just like in *The Office*,
we were busy pushing paper between games of online
poker, solitaire.

Now, so as not to be invisible, we stare into the green
light on our screens,
like dear, deceased John Prine, we sing to our neighbours,
'Hello in There'.
Sailors stuck in port, we grow tormented with an itch
for the remote,

our days pent-up but no longer spent in lath and plaster,
tied to counters,
nailed to benches, chained to desks. Shut in with
those we love, and those
we detest, we grow too familiar with each others' toilette
motions, a brown

and brawny company with bushy beards, an unshorn,
shabby set. Ishmael,
I'm in Stop & Shop, my glasses foggy with the breath my
homemade mask
directs upwards. I can't see the Rice Krispies from the
Cap'n Crunch,

the iceberg lettuce from the Boston Bibb. Call me, Ishmael!
Something wants
the heft of us to keep itself alive, cannot survive on
paper, cardboard, steel.
Invisible and indivisible, this fear we feel of it, which is the
water before

the breaching of the whale, that space where it's still
hearsay, hyperbole.
The dead pile up in refrigerated trucks and the street artist
paints rats
onto his bathroom walls, and, all aflutter as to whether
we're susceptible,

we monitor our sense of taste, our sense of smell. We hang
paper hearts up
in our storm windows and mark lintel and jamb with
the blood of a lamb
to keep at bay this chaos agent, this miniscule leviathan.
Our neighbours

have bought a boat and moved to Florida. We FaceTime
with them
as they sail the Intracoastal Waterway. I've even tried a
TikTok dance,
Ishmael, but my hips don't lie, I didn't stand a chance
against those lithe

young things, all twerk and vamp in the glow of your
iPhone. At dusk,
at a safe distance from one another, in order to drive
off the spleen,
we stroll, picking our teeth clean with halibut bones, or
flying drones

to capture footage of the shattered centres where, if a
pigeon wonders,
the pigeons wonder where we are. The atmosphere is better
without
our haste, Ishmael, and without our contrails now all
our aeroplanes

have come in to land, and the USNS *Comfort* rests where the cruise ships
used to sit at dock while their guests, by the busload, shopped at Saks
5th Ave. Ishmael, sometimes I think that this is really it — the breaking up

of the icebound stream of time, the universe going *kaput!* Let's put
the capstone on. Because casket upon casket piles up on the wharves
of Hart Island, where the mass grave's bulldozed in the potter's field,

and beds are laid out in the cathedral where, at Christmas, we carried
glasses of Merlot up and down the aisles and posed for photos, ridiculous
in our faux tuxedos. It's, as you say, a wicked world in all meridians

and yet we've grown fond of it, for all its flaws. Sentimental, as we loaf
and invite our souls, ringing our bells promptly at seven, singing 'Here
Comes the Sun'. Hit us up on WhatsApp, Ishmael. Find us on Zoom.

Shopping on eBay for Laika Memorabilia

Into the search engine I enter the five letters
of your name and wait for the image to appear —
a cigarette lighter that wears your face in
side profile and bas relief, as if you're some
sort of canine commissar, staring towards
the Kármán line of the future.
On ebay I'm scrolling through your afterlife:
a trinket box, a clock, a paperweight,
a postage stamp from the Emirate of Ajman.
How far you are now, little barker, from
your Moscow street hustle, the apparatchiks
with the sausage meat and tape measure.
Far as we are from the sickle and hammer
and football tops emblazoned CCCP,
Oleg Blokhin, or Andriy Bal maybe, scoring
in minute thirty three against the Brazil
of Oscar and Sócrates.

Did they use a catch-pole noose to entrap you?
Or did you come easily to their outstretched
hands, your tongue some fine grade
sandpaper against the first open palm
to offer food? Did you know, ever,
what was happening to you, strapped
to the vibrating table, or locked inside
a centrifuge and spun at ten times
the force of gravity? Then blasted
skyward from the Baikonur Cosmodrome
to celebrate the complex glories
of the Revolution? Your capsule up near
the rocket's nose looks, from here, like
an upended beer barrel — the one we stole
and rolled across three fields light years ago
but couldn't pry open. Carlsberg, I think,
or maybe Heineken.

I could have this puff-box for $160 plus postage
		and packing, or this pin badge for $24.99.
	A space dog postcard from 1985, or a copy
of *Life* with Belka and Strelka the cover stars
		and your sad story somewhere on the inside.
	Forgive me, Laika, if I sentimentalize your plight,
which calls to mind Robert Frost in a long,
		black Zim on his way to see Khrushchev, and
	an outfit near Santa Fe that, for a small fee, will blast
my ashes into space. Think outside the box,
		it says on their web page. And still we wish to know
	what you can teach us about weightlessness.
We're burdened, curious, for sure we are unsure
		on this fraught planet, where my vision
	begins to blur as I add to the watchlist
a commemorative coin from Mongolia, a set
		of nesting dolls from Azerbaijan.

Doctor Atomic

John Adams, 2005

I run my finger round the rim of a wineglass. If it's really cut crystal
it will sing, like the mezzo-soprano who, according to my playbill,
has played Olga in *Eugene Onegin*. It's 1945 in Los Alamos, while in
New York it's 2008, and in the space and time these lines would try

and fail to span you've moved to Thailand and are now back in Maine.
At the Met I've forgotten my glasses so it's only now I catch the opening
scene, where the table of elements is transformed to a series of mug-
shots that become the blinds the cast raise on a new dawn. I run my

finger round the rim of a wineglass and watch a rerun of the matinee.
Twelve years after the *Ding an sich* I wonder what it means to be
a citizen of this history in which the polyglot who reads the *Bhagavad-*
gita in the original Sanskrit is also the polyglot who drops the bomb.

I've memorized my rights and responsibilities while you've learned
the likes and dislikes of a king. Of 'a brilliant luminescence', Oppenheimer
sings, then he recites that sonnet by John Donne. And what the creators

want us to imagine is that none of this exists, that
the world ends

at the end of that hailstorm. No more the chandeliers
that were a gift
from Austria, no more, in the lush lobby, those
cantilevered stairs,
or the Chagall mural, where a boy with a horse's head
strums a lute
and a girl bursts from the body of a bird. I run my
finger round the rim

of a wineglass and imagine Lincoln Center blown to bits,
that you
and I never get to shoot the shit afterwards at Swift's
or The Stoned Crow,
where I'll admit I just don't get opera — why sing it when
so much
of what they sing is so mundane? On stage, the
bomb rests, snug

in its nest of electrics. 'At the sight of this, your shape
stupendous,'
the cast sing. The libretto is by a Peter Sellars, which
has me
humming *The Pink Panther* theme. It makes a sound like
trochee,
trochee, troch*ee*, as Colonel Tibbets opens the bomb
bay to unleash

Little Boy on Hiroshima, and Bernard Hoffman writes
to Wilson Hicks
of 'the sickly sweet smell of death'. We have come to
a knowledge

we can't unpick, so answer me this — is it wrong to want something
more for a swansong than a meteorologist singing the weather

and a general kvetching over his waistline? On the chalk-board, the men
record their bets on the outcome of the test in kilotons. The shadow
frozen onto the steps before a bank in that photograph from Getty
Images is the chalk outline at a crime scene in a century of crime. A half-

melted watch records the time as 8.15. I rub my finger round the rim
of a wineglass, which by the terms of this conceit is a fiction, as I am
before this screen, or in Row D Seat 115 of the Grand Tier, as Edward
Teller applies sunblock before everything's swallowed up into the glare.

You & Me: The B-Movie

In a universe where all logic is suspended, anything can happen.
— Robin Cross

1

All up to our elbows in salt and grease
we watch the screen as, once, we watched the sky,
await the alien inverse of our species
that looks like the monster from *Frankenstein*,
or comes disguised, dressed up as one of us,
albeit with a killer robot in tow
to warn us we flirt with apocalypse
as we worry our way to a tomorrow
that might mean giant ants or killer bees,
a tarantula or a deadly mantis
haunting the storm drains of Los Angeles,
feeding our wish for the ridiculous,
who go in fear of plague and the insect
and dress our fears in cheap special effects.

2

We dress our fears in cheap special effects
and seek our escape in far-fetched plot lines.
We're being invaded by the Planet X,
by this vegetable we'll be eaten alive.
Beware the ping-pong eyes of the vampire,
the teenage giant and the giant syringe,
the stun gun wielded by Zsa Zsa Gabor
who swears 'vimmen cannot live visout men,'
bottle blonde in *Queen of Outer Space*,
where everyone born male is in exile.
In the story of our species it is late
and while we're here we must believe a while

in gill-men rising from their black lagoon,
cat women from the dark side of the moon.

3

Cat women from the dark side of the moon —
even now they're plotting our demise.
Pod people are rising from their cocoons,
the future comes for us out of the black & white.
It wears an ill-fitting gorilla suit
or a helmet that looks like a human brain.
It speaks to an end we can't quite compute,
an end we're not ready to entertain.
Extraterrestrials touch down in Pleasantville,
'Them, Them, Them,' the mute girl suddenly screams
as doomsday and the diabolical
put on their glad rags and enter the scene.
All eyes ahead, mouths full of Jujubes,
we're watching the B-movie of you and me.

4

We're watching the B-movie of you and me,
a thrown together, low-budget affair
where the uncanny has us under siege
after Ed Wood sits in the director's chair
making flying saucers out of paper plates.
Beware those cloned Nazis from the Andes
and the long arm of the nebulous state.
Beware the future doused in kerosene
like those plates launched towards the camera
in *Planet 9 from Outer Space*, the final shot.

The future's all send up and chimera,
so bad it's good, so all we do is watch
until the credits fall, the contrast fades
on what might be the worst film ever made.

5

This might be the worst film ever made
with its loose script and jittery footage
made with cheap equipment, the actors paid
with promises of fame, minimum wage.
The monster's straight out of a pantomime;
inside the rubber suit there sweats a man.
The shoot ran over budget, out of time,
and for Venus or Mars it's Bronson Canyon
for a stand-in, just as it's radio static
for the crackle and whirr of this death ray
certain to prompt another gas panic.
Zombies are muscling in on our clambake,
and there's this swarm of fire-breathing flies,
amusing where they're meant to terrify.

6

Amusing where they're meant to terrify —
the shrinking man fleeing the family cat,
the fifty foot woman snagged on the power lines,
and hippies turned baldheaded maniacs
after a suspect batch of LSD.
Not even sprightly Steve McQueen can save us
in this, the B-movie of you and me.
All of our enemies are ambidextrous,

shape-shifters straight out of a comic strip,
amoeba with a taste for human flesh.
For a soundtrack it's this high-pitched music
played on a theremin and threatening to crush
our planet as it spins off its axis.
Imagine a world in which we don't exist.

7

Imagine a world in which we don't exist
as it says in the trailer voiceover.
Is it too late at this stage for a plot twist
as something touches us on the shoulder?
It could be the cold hand of Vincent Price
or Dean Parkin's one-eyed giant, full of rage —
whatever comes for us across the ice
to whom we're just a 'field of cabbages'.
The Plymouth rattles down a desert road;
inside, the sheriff and his deputy
outnumbered and with nowhere left to go
in the closing scene of this, our B-movie.
The End, it says. We stare at a bare screen,
all up to our elbows in salt and grease.

The Man Who Fell to Earth

Nicolas Roeg, 1976

In the opening shot the water level drops to reveal the ruins of a Mormon
settlement and all that remains of the cocaine trafficker turned government
snitch, or the mob boss who, at the Stardust, rigged the slots. A close-up

of something stuffed into a rust-pocked oil barrel. A close-up of a B-29
Superfortress, one of the largest aircraft used in World War II. And, yes,
you're correct, this is not the film the marquee promised you, or at least

it isn't yet. And if it's into Lake Mead that David Bowie plummets in homage
to Bruegel's *Landscape with the Fall of Icarus* then I'm pretty sure he'd break
his pretty neck. Bowie in a herringbone overcoat. Bowie in a Homburg or

Panama hat. Cocaine Bowie twitchy on Dick Cavett, tapping against the floor
his walking stick. Which one is your favourite? Go ahead, pick, as the drought
on his planet becomes the bathtub ring around the Hoover Dam, where,

once, those men known as high scalers — ex-circus performers, many
of them — swung on ropes down the sides of the canyon to work free

the loose stone. And it's out of their weekends that Las
Vegas grows,

the Apache and the Flamingo, Liberace at the Riviera
and the Rat Pack
at the Sands. Out of the dream of flood control for the
farmers of Colorado
and the blue prints of Frank 'Hurry Up' Crowe. The
first hard hat a fedora

dipped in molten tar, and the rocks falling like a shower of
meteors.
At its base, the weight of the dam water would one day
be roughly equal
to five elephants standing on your head, its volume enough
to submerge

Connecticut to a depth of ten feet. And I'm guessing
this must be
what Bowie sees on TV from his faraway home, for which
White
Sands National Park will serve as a stand-in. I like
him in a sun visor

and tennis gear playing ping-pong beneath a chandelier. I
like him
in his dentist's chair, watching a stack of analogue
screens. On one
a woman dances in white lingerie. On another two beach
boys throw

back and forth a frisbee in what could well be an ad
for Coppertone.
I like the moment in the bathroom where he tweezers out
his one

blue and his one brown eye to reveal the orange eyes
of a reptile,

and how your brother's ex joked, as we watched in their
New Hampshire
basement, or during a heatwave in Texas on a new
widescreen, that soon
enough we'll be the aliens, crash-landing somewhere,
desperate for a drink.

Close Encounters

The spaceship appeared to him on the road in
from New Lake, or so went the rumour. *E.T.* was on
at the Astor, while on a neighbour's TV it was
Close Encounters. My father was like
an alien that year in his clogs and orange flares,
that unkempt head of curls that meant
he always got stopped at the border, pulled over
under the shadow of the watchtower.
At school the *máistir* extended his telescopic
pointer so we could follow the fleet around the globe —
the *Irish Oak* in the Sea of Japan, the *Irish Cedar*
in the Gulf of Mexico. In the playground
he was a running joke, the space cadet
who'd attached a forty foot antenna
to the roof of the family home, though later,
on ham radio, he would explain a failed coup
to a cosmonaut on Mir.

We were a town of characters. The drunk-
on-dole-day-pioneer-pin-wearer falling asleep
over his soup in the café. The one we called
Oisín, though Seamus was his name, teaching
a girl half his age to *cha-cha-cha*. And our
sci-fi obsessed bachelor, his ear cocked
for the music of the spheres. Once, in a long
since defunct hardware store, he sold my father
a church organ that would not stay in tune.
It was a present for my mother, who wanted
her children to learn piano, or wanted us
to be one of those families where the children
learn piano. Those years we were poor.
We took the carpets up from one house
and tried to make them fit in another. My mother
embroidered the crest onto my knock-
off school jumper.

I got lines for staring out the window.
    Even then I was a daydreamer. It's raining
outside the prefabs where Mrs Toye is
        telling us about her Russian adventures, and
    I wish a tractor beam would reach down
and pluck me out of there. On the way home
I'll stop in at Mary Eoin's for a Mars Bar.
    And our man, who may as well have been from Mars?
        Watch him now as the headlights on his car
    are caught up in the glare of adventure,
a glow like the glow in those religious posters
        that yellow above the counter as Mary roots
    through a drawer for change to my pound note.
They're both long gone into the earth, the ether,
    and so who cares if what he sees is no more
        than one of those tricks that light and loneliness
    play on the mind up here?

Roach

Hard to believe it could go a week
   headless before, lacking a mouth,
it dies of thirst — this little gadabout
   in the reddish brown tailcoat, that
materializes when I hit the lights. And
   I'm thinking of Kafka's bug piece now,
(aren't you?) as I pursue it with a copy
   of *The New Yorker,* rolled up like
that strip torn from a Rizzla packet
   to make a filter for a funny cigarette.
It 'came to me in my misery, lying
   in bed,' Franz writes to Felice, whom he
will never wed. He hopes to publish
   it quickly but there's the war. French
reinforcements clatter to the front.
   The first chlorine attack occurs at
the Battle of Ypres. Gregor's metamorphosis
   manifests his abasement, I'll read
later in our basement apartment
   in the northwest Bronx, where our
landlord keeps his Rottweilers tied
   up outside the door. 'They'll get used
to you,' he reassures, but they don't.

   Something stirs under the fluorescence
in the bedroom, carries on the spines
   of its legs some remnant of the sewer,
and I'm chasing the latest of our uninvited
   guests through the lopsided doors
of the armoire until it disappears, or
   I'm standing outside Roche's Stores
with my dog Rex as my mother rises
   on the escalator, off on her yearly
quest for American tan tights, and, if
   I've behaved myself, a little pick 'n' mix.

Did you know that to cure tetanus
the body of a roach was once ground
into a loose leaf tea? Did you know
that in the trenches at Aisne one of
the main agents of chaos was the flea?
I slip my feet into my Asics unknowingly.
Into the grinder I drop these Arabica
beans, then brew the coffee I'll pitch
across the floor, when I start to sense
that half-squashed space invader's writhe
and wriggle, its rock and roll, between
the insole of my sneaker and my big toe.

The Making of Jaws

Not the tank behind the studio this time. Instead, the open water
    of the sound, the script still being written as the scenes are filmed,
and no one, it seems, ready to get us out of this one — not the aqua-

    phobic police chief or the sleazeball mayor who, in a summer town,
worries over summer dollars. The soundtrack oscillates between
    E and F until the D bites down, and the camera skirts the surface

of the water so that it feels as if we're about to drown. Richard Dreyfuss
    looks so much like my father the year he worked at the fish farm. I untie
the dinghy from the quay, and we splutter out into the sea again. I cut

    the belly of this *Carcharodon carcharias* open and find, not just
these half-digested tommy cots and this crushed can of Narragansett,
    but also John Locke's definition of consciousness as the 'perception

of what passes in a man's own mind', and the psychiatrist, later to
    perish in Auschwitz, who defines *anxiété* as this dark and distressing
feeling of expectation. The lobster writhes in its buoy-marked trap.

In their ringed enclosure the salmon flash their bellies of chainmail.
And something reaches up for us its hand of vulcanized rubber, as
in *Creature from the Black Lagoon*. ‘Farewell and adieu to you,

fair Spanish ladies,’ Robert Shaw sings as the Orca putters out, off and
away. It’s a nod to the *Pequod* and Ahab’s fate. As with the snare-shaped
jawbone through which the scene is filmed it’s a means of telling us

he won’t be coming home. So let’s forget the shark, it’s stiff jaws
and crooked teeth that we don’t get to see until at least an hour in.
It’s the anticipation of the thing and not the thing itself that ends up

being the making of the film. The sea takes her own, as someone must
have said way back in that way back when, when the tide belched up
a fisherman who’d never learned to swim. I cut the outboard and

drift back into it again, how the local shopkeeper ran his Doberman
beside his blue sedan, and the mobile butcher carried to our kitchen
door a bucket of bull’s blood, a Christmas gift for a loyal customer.

I cut the outboard and raise from the cutting room floor
 that scene
 where, in an almost empty theatre, Shaw's character
 laughs his way
through a matinee showing of John Huston's take on
 Melville's tale,

 and something enters the swim of the right brain that's
 way more
sinister than the animatronic creature the crew nickname
 Bruce
 that, on the first day of the shoot, sinks to the bottom
 of the bay.

Circus, Fire

The big cat act was over, and The Great Wallendas were
getting ready to work
on the high wire. Not yet Arthur Konyot and his
Hungarian Riders. Not yet

Lou Jacobs emerging from the cramped quarters of his
clown car. And let's
say you and I have just wandered in from the
midway with a red balloon,

a monkey sewn from rabbit fur. Let's say the circus has
arrived a day late
from Providence, the big top coated in paraffin wax
to keep out the rain.

Not yet the cigarette dropped outside the men's toilets, or
the match struck
by a razorback livid over late pay, or the schizo-
phrenic who would confess

later to setting the blaze at the behest of a ghost in a head-
dress. Not yet
the stench of burning flesh in this, another century
of needless death,

setting off the vet who remembers Okinawa, where an
enemy soldier
burns at the end of a flame-thrower. Instead, we're in
the year of Liz Taylor

in *National Velvet* and Bing Crosby asking 'Would you like
to swing on a star?'
And my father, a year after this not-yet-fire, slipping
out between the legs

of his mother, which means, of course, we can't really be
there, in the third
row of the grandstand, waiting for Emmett Kelly
to hang his tattered coat

on the tightrope and beat himself at a game of solitaire,
for Dolly Copeland
to slip from her slop shoes on the sawdust track
that circles those three rings

before taking to the air. Yet there we are, among the families
of those men
from Travelers Insurance and Royal Typewriter and,
by the bleachers,

the ex-servicemen in their wheelchairs, all of us come to see
the elephants,
which in the parlance of the place means to lose your
innocence. Not yet

the mahouts afloat on their howdahs, the horses testing the
length of their
lunge lines, and Kelly's 'Weary Willie' chewing a
cabbage on the sidelines,

or, with a broom, sweeping up the spotlight. Not yet my
father's father
come back from Egypt and the war with a deep tan,
my father's father

back from the South of France singing 'It's a Long Way to
Tipperary' or
'We'll Meet Again'. Not yet, but soon, Karl Wallenda
in San Juan falling

to his death between the penthouse suites of the Condado
and the Flamboyan,
and the heat that pops your red balloon, the heat like
wasp stings on the skin

as the tent takes flame like a Zeppelin over the city of our
dreams. And the fire
like the last blast of a sunset, and the fire like the
onset of a full moon.

Fresh Air

The bats drop to the cave floor like a dirty wash and, in
 the sea,
  it gets harder to make a shell as my foot hovers
   between the brake
and gas pedal in the parking garage at Hartford Hospital,
 where

  depending on where the car is between floors, it's either
   static
on the radio or NPR. Static on the radio or NPR, and
 you've been
  with us only a few hours here in New England's Rising
   Star, where

the snow falls on the South End and Frog Hollow as Terry
 Gross talks
  to Elizabeth Kolbert. It whites out the white lines down
   the middle
of the road. It frosts, then sugarcoats the frozen pond in the
 park

  named for Colonel Albert Pope, while guest and host
   discuss
a brown tree snake in Guam that has no enemies, a yellow
 frog
  in Panama that was a lucky charm. And the children,
   who didn't

especially want it to happen, still skating at the edge of
 Auden's
  poem, and in that painting by Bruegel the Elder, upright
   forever
on their skates of bone. Away they go between the starlings
 and

the house sparrows, and those bird traps that,
according to
the allegory some see, are baits of the devil for the careless
soul.
I've brought a bag of diapers and a change of clothes,
the car seat

in which we'll take you home through the snow that won't
take no
for an answer, the snow writing its own erasure poem.
The signal
comes back and then it goes. 'This is *Fresh Air*. I'm Terry
Gross.'

The meteorologist says the weather 'calls for', as if the
weather
has a mind of its own. And I wonder, heir to all we are and
what
little we possess, what we've signed you up for, bringing
you here,

everything bathed in this pinkish glow like my printout
(the ink
cartridge was low) of that Flemish village of sky and ice
and ice
and snow, that frozen river from five hundred years ago. Hats

and scarves, spinning tops and hockey sticks, and how
the more
I look the more I start to see you in the scene as that boy
raising
the leg he's just pushed off with, maybe, or the one who
huffs

and puffs after a wayward puck. I'm your father, Aengus,
looking
for an empty spot, and shit out of luck, as, on your
mother's arm,
the nurse inflates a pressure cuff, and the orderly carries
a cake

to the room where you've just woken up, 'congrat-
ulations' written
in green cursive on the buttercream, which looks just
like this
snow burying everything as we get lost in the
Anthropocene.

The Vegas Nerve

While trying to put a finger
   on the source of what ails me —
this flutter in my chest that
   seems to augur cardiac arrest,
or at least signal a blockage
   of the aorta — my doctor has me
thinking of Elvis near the end,
   of rhinestone and amphetamine,
a penthouse suite at the top
   of the Westgate, since when
he says vagus I hear Vegas,
   which sets me going like a slot
machine, or the preacher
   at an Elvis-themed wedding,
and now I'm thinking of
   the newborn king billed as
an extra added attraction,
   sandwiched between Freddie
Martin and his Orchestra
   and the unique comic stylings
of Shecky Greene. It's 1956.
   He's twenty-one, which means
my parents have yet to meet
   in that guest house on Achill
Island, have yet to marry
   in Belfast and the chaos of '69.
'My Dad's becoming a robot,'
   our son explained last week
to his preschool teacher after
   he spied the Holter monitor
under my striped Tee, trying to
   calibrate my blips and beats.
And, look, I know it sounds
   ridiculous, but sometimes,
I swear, it's as if my heart just

quits. Others it seems to wish
to put a fist clean through
my chest as if to say, 'See,
Mister, I'm all that's between us
and a flat line.' And it's the heart
that'll give up on Elvis in time,
the autopsy suggesting Quaaludes,
and codeine. By then, he'll be
the face on the mug from which
my uncle drinks his tea, a 45
with a first line I like to repeat,
curling my upper lip, singing
how it's one for the money,
and two for the show. This is how
Vegas enters our sitting room,
so too with Honolulu, Acapulco.
I go back to where the cathodes
don't quite meet — Elvis on O'ahu
singing 'aloha' from a jeep,
Elvis getting busy on a trapeze,
while the doctor describes
the vagus nerve as a highway
that runs, like memory maybe,
between the gut and brain.
It's like Vegas only in that it has
something to do with touch
and taste. It's like Vegas only
in that it can, in a flutter, lead
the heart astray. And I'm not
ready yet to leave this building.
Later, the nurse will dry shave
my chest and I'll run in place,
hooked up to a twelve-lead ECG.
Later, I'll listen to Elvis sing
'Bridge Over Troubled Water'

just a little off-key. For now though,
   I'm stripped to my boxer briefs
as the doctor listens into me
   through the stethoscope's cold
steel, and I hear in his hypothesis
   for what might be amiss, a word
that suggests its opposite.

Guess Who's Coming to Dinner

Stanley Kramer, 1967

I could so easily go all Hollywood on this, as in that giddy
opening scene
from Kramer's film, where the smiling couple step off
their plane from Hawaii
and the terminal fills with the sugar of the theme. 'You've
got to live a little,'

Jacqueline Fontaine sings, and I picture my mother
there in a middle row
at the Odeon or the Ambassador, the Grand Opera House
maybe or the ABC,
where, by way of rear projection, we're riding shotgun
in the car that carries

Katharine Houghton and Sidney Poitier. Outside the
picture palace it's Belfast
in late '67 or early '68. It's the beginning of the new
imbroglio, although you
wouldn't guess it as we skim the San Francisco hills on our
way to the Drayton

residence. My mother's tired of explaining quadratic
equations, the coefficient,
the variable, the constant term. On the ride over she slips
between the lines,
daydreams of the man from across the water she'll
marry in August of '69.

In the washed-out photograph that hangs in my office they
stand on the steps
of Saint Teresa's church. The unremarkable black suit,
the obligatory white dress —

my parents on their wedding day in the riots. But let's not go there yet. Up on

the screen it's Katharine Hepburn and Spencer Tracy together for the last time,
it's Mel's Diner, fresh Oregon boysenberry sugar ice-cream, Isabel Sanford
declaring 'Civil rights is one thing, this here is something else' when

John Wade Prentice shows up on that ivory terrace in what must be Nob Hill
or Pacific Heights. I think of my father and grandfather filling their pipes
with Old Road and Walnut Plug, how he always addressed him as Mr Flynn,

of the cuckoo clock that erupts to mark the hour in that front room, where
the wedding guests squeeze in after the reception hall burns down in all that
fire and brimstone, after the best man gets stranded somewhere between Belfast

and Lisburn, so that our smiling couple marry with borrowed rings. The light
falls across my mother's face. 'As long as there's the two of us,' Miss Fontaine
sings, in a jazz club this time. And it's only now it dawns on me that, in this story,

my mother must see something of her own. At the intermission she'll order
Butterkist popcorn, or a Lyons Maid King Cone. After the credits roll she'll take

the bus home in the pissing rain. In a phone box, with
someone knocking to get in,

she'll drop her last fifty pence into the slot and the operator
will connect her
to this man from another place, another faith, with
whom she'll play out
her own version of the theme. Around a round table now
I picture them,

saying please pass the potatoes, please pass the greens,
and the calf's liver
that does not come to my grandmother by way of some
be-bopping butcher boy
in a red beret. Like I said, I could go all Hollywood
on this, if I haven't already.

Evel Knievel

Although the TV's black & white it's in colour I see
my ten-year-old self on the edge of the corduroy settee

as, coming to you live from where memory yields to myth —
you know that coliseum, you know that Cow Palace

in which a man, who is part Elvis and part Icarus,
will jump a row of Matchbox cars or Pepsi trucks,

cutting the air in half on the Harley or Triumph
he's revving on the takeoff ramp, ready to jump

in Kellogg, Idaho, let's say, or Portland, Oregon,
where his cape, spangled with stars, flaps in the wind

as, in a sudden rush of gears, the descent begins
that will or won't propel him across that grand canyon,

the stadium all flashbulbs as he cuts a crooked line,
trying to cross, like me, between two points in time.

The Comb Over

Neck flush with a cleft in the porcelain,
    it all starts to move backwards down the drain,
    some Coriolis effect setting me down
        in Errigal Stores, where
    the owner stoops to the soft-serve
machine. Spearmint and Juicy Fruit.
Tayto and King. How the last
        strands, teased to a swirl
    above his tonsured crown, come loose
    as he sinks a Flake
        into my ninety-nine.
I separate the remnants of it again,
    run it back through the comb
    this midweek afternoon in SEI Salon.
        The penny sweets beside the register.
    The pencil behind his ear. How,
round here, I'm known as 'Kirin,
like the beer,' which translates
    roughly as 'Monsieur Giraffe'.
        As Mitsumi works my scalp
    to a lather she speaks

of fishing trips, movies she's seen —
    Seu Jorge in *The Life Aquatic*, a striped bass
    off Montauk, or the Jersey Shore.
        On her fingers there's the last
      of an American Spirit
or a Lucky Strike, under their tips
my skull's topography of bone,
        like a stone worked
    gradually smooth by rain. I slip
    a five-pound note across
        the red Formica counter.
I run my tongue over what drips,
    vanilla, from a cone. Back and forth

I go, like a man trying to make
the most of a side parting
in spite of the insistence
of time and tine. Head hovering over
the sink, like one condemned,
I steel myself now and as the blade
comes down to reveal the full
extent of the recession.

My brow clear-cuts a path towards my crown,
where the vertex expands
as if in praise of the sun. I fuss and fret
over diminishing returns, thinking
of monks, the so-called
barcode men of Japan,
and that cruise-ship waiter I worked with
one summer in Eastbourne,
who must decide again
whether to work starboard or port
based on where the wind
will keep in place his comb over. Midway
through my life's journey,
or slightly further on, I find myself
adrift in the stylist's chair.
At my neck the teeth of the clippers,
at my feet these grey flecks of hair
as, to show me the cut, Mitsumi
holds one mirror up to another,
making this vortex
into which I disappear.

Eat the Peach

Peter Ormrod, 1986

So, anticlockwise, we go back to where, anticlockwise, these two
carefree-for-an-instant characters circle, on motor-bikes, this plywood
cylinder, this circus ring. Think flamingos coming in to land, or
water washing backwards down a drain, and you'll have the shape

of them, there on the Bog of Allen as they ascend. They've seen
Elvis do this in *Roustabout*, they like to repeat his lines — 'You ought
to stop reading those hotrod magazines, buddy, cycle is out,
it's either bike or motorcycle!' Now I repeat theirs, turning

anticlockwise to where, in the front row of the Classic Cinema,
I watch the movie with a boy I barely know. This is Cooperation
North and he's my host, twenty of us having crossed the border
so twenty of them can come the other way. He speaks so softly

and so South Derry that I can barely understand a word he says.
He'll leave our house believing my father's a carpenter, that he
did all the woodwork up at Glenveagh. His name's John Anthony

as my father's name is Anthony John. We suck on
straws. Into bags

of crisps we sink our hands as, in a country & western
suit
and Stetson this rhinestone cowboy shows up on
the screen
to suggest the bikers might smuggle Smirnoff and
cigarettes
north to south in order to finance their sideshow
scheme.

And I'm seeing now, though I can't see then, that the
entire
film's an uncomplicated ode — a drinking hole
called The Frontier,
a very local obsession with the quiffed, coiffed, mutton-
chopped
king, this would-be impresario, who speaks in a
voice halfway

between James Cagney and John Wayne. Boots is his
name,
or his nickname, I should say, and he's never
ventured west
of the Shannon. It's 1986 or '87, the year myself and
Anthony
John, in our Lada Riva, come to a halt before the
Customs post

where he'll show a false receipt for the snooker table —
not
a 12′ x 6′ but a 6′ x 3′ — we've secured to the roof
rack with

bungee cords. I rack the reds and set the colours on their spots:
yellow, brown and green; blue, pink and black. I turn anticlockwise

to where, in their flat caps, jean jackets, and anoraks, a crowd
gathers around the Wall of Death, and the band breaks into song.
Soon we'll go back to John Anthony's home in his contractor father's
Ford Escort Mark I, John Anthony Senior joking about the soldier

who pulls us over putting on an accent to pretend he's not from
here, as later, mistaking one of our number, whose last name
is Mooney, for a follower of Sun Myung Moon, he'll suggest all
cult members should be put on a small island and burned.

On the radio it's Charley Pride with 'The Snakes Crawl at Night',
then it's Joe Dolan with 'Suspicious Minds'. When he asks about
the film Junior describes the scene where, before the frightened
audience abandons them, one man on his Honda begins to climb,

anticlockwise, while his sidekick describes what's going on, talking

about himself in the third person — 'And now Artie
will join Vinnie
in a dual demonstration involving two machines.' Think
of the dice
alive inside a roulette wheel, or lost coins tumbling
in a tumble dryer,

think of the unlikeliness of our staying put on this planet
of ours as it
spins, anticlockwise, at a rate of a thousand miles per
hour. It's 1986
or '87, and I've no idea yet what the title of the film means.
Like Boots,
I've never been to these United States, and I've no
interest in going.

Acknowledgements and Notes

Acknowledgements are due to the editors of the following publications where some of these poems, or versions of them, were published first: *Action-Spectacle, Alaska Quarterly Review, American Poetry Review, Arts & Letters, The Cincinnati Review, Crazyhorse, Eamon at 80: Celebrating Eamon Grennan, The Georgia Review, Hampden-Sydney Poetry Review, The Hartford Courant, Notre Dame Review, Poetry Ireland Review, Poetry London, Southword, The Southern Review* and *The Stinging Fly.*

Many thanks to Peter Fallon and everyone at The Gallery Press, to my fellow poets Ryan Black, Colin Cheney, James Ciano, Matt Donovan, Kathleen Graber, Eamon Grennan, and Clare Rossini for their kindness, encouragement, and good company, to my generous colleagues in the English Department at Trinity College in Hartford, Connecticut, and most of all to Hope, Leo and Aengus.

page 11 The episode of *The Twilight Zone* referred to here is 'Where Is Everybody?' (1959). The first two lines of the second stanza are adapted from Allen Ginsberg's 'Howl'. The exchange between Stephen and Davin is from James Joyce's *A Portrait of the Artist as a Young Man.* The quote from Jacob Steendam appears in *Gotham* by Edwin G Burrows and Mike Wallace. The story of the man who rode to town carrying wheat on his shoulders so as not to burden his horse, which also appears in *Gotham*, originally featured in a jest book titled *Merie Tales of the mad men of Gotam* (c. 1565).

page 14 The Franciscan Complex is a geologic term for the heterogeneous rocks found along the coast of Northern California. The Chinatown Fair Family Fun Center on Mott Street in New York was once home to a tic-tac-toe playing chicken named Lillie.

page 16 Slavoj Žižek described *Underground* as 'one of the most horrible films I've seen' in a September 2008 conversation with Bernard-Henri Lévy at the New York Public Library. The Ted Hughes quote is from the opening of the title poem in *Wodwo.*

page 19 The Emma Lazarus poem referred to here is 'The New Colossus'. The Allen Ginsberg biography referenced is Barry Miles's *Allen Ginsberg: A Biography*. Frédéric Auguste Bartholdi was the French painter and sculptor who designed the Statue of Liberty.

page 24 The Jean Toomer novel referred to here is *Cane* (1923).

page 27 Joe F Weber wrote the lyrics and music to 'If You Can't Be True to the Red, White, and Blue, Then Go Back Where You Belong'. Atlanta Braves pitcher, John Rocker, referred to New York Mets fans as 'degenerates' in a December 1999 interview with *Sports Illustrated*. The Guardian Angels are a civilian 'crime-watch group' established in 1979.

page 30 The quote from Antoine Yates comes from an April 2020 *New York Times* article by Corey Kilgannon titled 'A 425-Pound Tiger Living in a Harlem Apartment? Yes, It Happened.' Edmund Burke's description of the sublime is from *A Philosophical Enquiry into the Origin of our Ideas of the Sublime and Beautiful* (1757). The name of the wildlife sanctuary in Ohio where Ming the tiger was resettled is Noah's Lost Ark.

page 33 In his essay 'Fate' Ralph Waldo Emerson writes, 'The German and Irish millions, like the Negro, have a great deal of guano in their destiny. They are ferried over the Atlantic and carted over America, to ditch and to drudge, to make corn cheap and then to lie down permanently.' The description of the congressman's 'man-bulge' comes from a 2011 article in *iPolitics*.

page 36 The Amato Opera was opened by Antonio and Sally Amato in 1948. From 1964 until its closing in 2009 it was located on the Bowery a few doors down from CBGB. The opera referenced here is Mozart's *Don Giovanni*. The Bernard Malamud quote is from his novel *The Tenants* (1971).

page 39 *The Onion* published an article in May 2015 under the headline 'Toyota Recalls 1993 Camry Due To Fact That Owners Really Should Have Bought Something New By Now.'

page 43 Thomas Ridge was the US Secretary of Homeland Security 2003-2005. Van Cortlandt Park in Riverdale, New York, is named after the Van Cortlandt family. Pierre Van Cortlandt was, in the late 1700s, lieutenant to New York State Governor George Clinton.

page 45 *Complex* magazine's countdown of the fifty worst special effects in movie history appears in a November 2012 article by Matt Barone.

page 48 Most of the photographs in question appeared in a March 2011 issue of *The Atlantic*. The epigraph is from a January 2013 article titled 'Do Animals in Chernobyl's Fallout Zone Glow?'

page 50 Known as the father of cryonics, Robert Ettinger was the author of *The Prospect of Immortality* (1962). The illusionist referred to here is David Blaine. Along with Oprah Winfrey he is quoted from a preshow interview in April 2008. The phrase 'wee tim'rous beastie' is adapted from 'To a Mouse' by Robert Burns.

page 53 George A Romero describes horror movies as parables in a 2008 interview with the American Film Institute. '*Aujord'hui maman est morte*' is the opening sentence to Albert Camus's novel, *L'Étranger* (1942). A report on the culled mink rising from a mass grave in Jutland appeared in *The Guardian* on 25 November 2020.

page 56 Several phrases from Herman Melville's *Moby-Dick* (1851) feature here. I owe the title to my colleague, David Rosen.

page 61 This poem is for Colin Cheney. The letter quoted here was sent by photographer, Bernard Hoffman, to *Life* magazine editor, Wilson Hicks, on 3 September 1945. The photograph of the frozen shadow is not credited.

page 64 The epigraph is from Robin Cross's *B Movies* (1981). The quote in section 3 is from *Them!* (1954). The quote in section 7 is from *The Thing from Another World* (1951).

page 73 The quote from Franz Kafka appears in a letter (17 November 1912) to his fiancée Felice Bauer.

page 75 John Locke's definition of consciousness appears in *An Essay Concerning Human Understanding* (1689). The psychiatrist referenced here is Joseph Lévy-Valensi.

page 78 The Hartford Circus fire killed one hundred and sixty-seven spectators and injured seven hundred others on 6 July 1944. I'm grateful to Michael Skidgell for his book *The Hartford Circus Fire* (2014) and to www.circusfire1944.com.

page 81 *Fresh Air* is a weekday interview show on National Public Radio in the US. The painting referred to here is Pieter Bruegel the Elder's *Winter Landscape with Skaters and Bird Trap* (1565).

page 93 Cooperation North was a cross-border peace-building organization that facilitated meetings between secondary school students during the Troubles in Northern Ireland.